We Read
PHONICS™

Ant in Her Pants

TREASURE BAY

ENJOY!

Paul
Orshoski

Parent's Introduction

Welcome to **We Read Phonics**! This series is designed to help you assist your child in reading. Each book includes a story, as well as some simple word games to play with your child. The games focus on the phonics skills and sight words your child will use in reading the story.

Here are some recommendations for using this book with your child:

1 Word Play

There are word games both before and after the story. Make these games fun and playful. If your child becomes bored or frustrated, play a different game or take a break.

Phonics is a method of sounding out words by blending together letter sounds. However, not all words can be "sounded out." **Sight words** are frequently used words that usually cannot be sounded out.

② Read the Story

After some word play, read the story aloud to your child—or read the story together, by reading aloud at the same time or by taking turns. As you and your child read, move your finger under the words.

Next, have your child read the entire story to you while you follow along with your finger under the words. If there is some difficulty with a word, either help your child to sound it out or wait about five seconds and then say the word.

③ Discuss and Read Again

After reading the story, talk about it with your child. Ask questions like, "What happened in the story?" and "What was the best part?" It will be helpful for your child to read this story to you several times. Another great way for your child to practice is by reading the book to a younger sibling, a pet, or even a stuffed animal!

The funniest part was when she went to the vet!

LEVEL **3** **Level 3** introduces words with long "a" and long "i" (as in *late* and *like*), as well as the vowel combinations "er," "ir," and "ur" (as in *her, sir,* and *fur*). Other letter combinations include "qu" (as in *quick*), "sh" (as in *shine*), "th" (as in *math*), "ch" (as in *church*), and "tch" (as in *match*).

Ant in Her Pants

A We Read Phonics™ Book

Level 3

Text Copyright © 2010 by Treasure Bay, Inc.
Illustrations Copyright © 2010 by Jeffrey Ebbeler

Reading Consultants: Bruce Johnson, M.Ed., and Dorothy Taguchi, Ph.D.

We Read Phonics™ is a trademark of Treasure Bay, Inc.

Published by Treasure Bay, Inc.
P.O. Box 119
Novato, CA 94948 USA

Printed in Malaysia

Library of Congress Catalog Card Number: 2009929514

ISBN: 978-1-60115-328-9

Visit us online at:
www.TreasureBayBooks.com

PR-11-17

Ant in Her Pants

By Paul Orshoski

Illustrated by Jeffrey Ebbeler

Word Bingo

Playing a game with these words will help your child read the story.

Materials:

Option 1—Fast and Easy: To print the game materials from your computer, go online to www.WeReadPhonics.com, then go to this book title and click on the link to "View & Print: Game Materials."

Option 2—Make Your Own: You'll need 12 index cards, paper or cardboard, ruler, scissors, and colored markers or crayons. Write each of these words on an index card:

thud pants shock lunch when hurt
grant wire turn slacks gave never

Then create some Bingo cards with your child. Each player can make his or her own card. Start with making a 4 by 4 or 5 by 5 grid. Fill the grid with random words from above. Words can be used more than once. Then, create some colored dots to put over the words.

1 Mix the word cards and place them face down. A card is turned over and the word is read.

2 Players put a dot on the words on their Bingo card if matched. If the word appears more than once on a card, put a dot on each one.

3 The first player to complete a row, across, up and down, or diagonally, wins the game.

4 Play again!

Sight Word Game

Memory

Was!

OK, now pick another card.

This is a fun way to practice recognizing some sight words used in the story.

Materials:

Option 1—Fast and Easy: To print the game materials from your computer, go online to www.WeReadPhonics.com, then go to this book title and click on the link to "View & Print: Game Materials."

Option 2—Make Your Own: You'll need 18 index cards and a marker. Write each word listed on the right on two cards. You will now have two sets of cards.

1 Using one set of cards, ask your child to repeat each word after you. Shuffle both decks of cards together, and arrange the cards face down in a grid pattern.

2 The first player turns over one card and says the word, then turns over a second card and says the word. If the cards match, the player takes those cards and continues to play. If they don't match, both cards are turned over, and it's the next player's turn.

3 Keep the cards. You can make more cards with other **We Read Phonics** books and combine the cards for even bigger games!

was

she

said

where

down

herself

so

were

of

Miss Grant got an
ant in her pants.

It came up her sock…

…and gave her a shock.

It ate her sack lunch…

…then went for her punch.

It ran to her chin…

…where it sat with a grin.

It ran down her back,
then fled to her slacks.

It hurt when it bit.
Miss Grant had a fit.

She felt a sharp burn…

…so she made a quick turn.

She ran in the mud…

...then fell with a thud.

She hit a hot wire.

Her pants were on fire.

She got herself wet...

…and went to the vet.

He said she was ill…

…and gave her a pill.

The pill did not help.
And so she still rants...

…that she never got rid
of the ant in her pants.

Can you think of another word that rhymes with ant?

I can't.

Very good!

Rhyming

Practicing rhyming words helps children learn how words are similar.

1. Explain to your child that these words rhyme because they have the same end sounds: *ant, can't, pant, Grant, rant,* and *chant.*

2. Ask your child to say a word that rhymes with *ant.*

3. If your child has trouble, offer some possible answers or repeat step 1. It's okay to accept nonsense words, for example, *gant.*

4. When your child is successful, repeat step 2 with these words:

   back   (possible answers: *Jack, lack, knack, pack, rack, sack, stack, tack*)

   wire   (possible answers: *fire, higher, liar, tire, buyer*)

   lunch   (possible answers: *bunch, hunch, munch, punch*)

   her   (possible answers: *fur, were, sir, purr, spur, stir*)

   wet   (possible answers: *bet, fret, get, jet, let, met, net, pet, set*)

   mine   (possible answers: *fine, line, nine, twine, pine, sign, vine*)

   gave   (possible answers: *cave, Dave, grave, pave, rave, slave, wave*)

Phonics Game

Making Words

Creating words using certain letters will help your child read this story.

Materials: thick paper or cardboard; pencil, crayon or marker; scissors

1 Cut 2 x 2 inch squares from the paper or cardboard and print these letters and letter combinations on the squares: a, e, i, o, u, ch, ck, sh, ur, ir, er, b, c, d, g, h, k, l, n, q, r, s, t, v, *and* w.

2 Place the cards letter side up in front of your child.

3 Ask your child to make as many words as possible that end with "-ave." Give him or her these ending letters ("a," "v," and "e"), and ask your child to make words by adding letters to the beginning. Words could include *wave, cave, gave, rave, Dave,* and *shave.*

4 Do the same with these ending-letter combinations: "-ant," "-ock," "-ire," "-urn," "-ake," *and* "-ack."

5 Your child can also make other words using any of the letters or letter combinations available.

If you liked **Ant in Her Pants,**
here is another **We Read Phonics**™ book you are sure to enjoy!

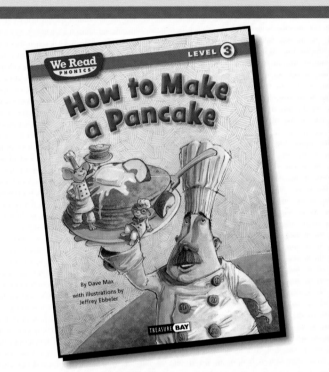

How to Make a Pancake

Making pancakes has never been more fun! Join a wild chef and two mice as they show how simple it is to make a big stack of delicious pancakes. The book is easy to read and filled with lots of humor for young readers!